Seagift 2024

Seagift 2024

Edited by Miriam Wei Wei Lo and Alison Dench

Sheridan Institute of Higher Education

CONTENTS

CONTENTS

Introduction

Welcome to the second issue of *Seagift*: an initiative of the Creative Writing team at Sheridan Institute of Higher Education.

We delight, once more, in this collection of stories and poems that have arrived on our shores. *Seagift* was chosen as a name to evoke the ocean and its gifts: bladderwrack, sea urchins, and abalone shells—tossed onto the shore; so apparently random, like life and art—a disorderly order. We hope to echo one of the ancient creation stories, held by both Jewish and Christian traditions, that depicts God as Spirit hovering over the face of the deep, preparing to do the work of calling this universe into being. Elements from this tradition are also present in the Islamic creation story where the throne of God sits above the water before the world is made.

Seagift acknowledges the Indian Ocean location of Sheridan in Boorloo/Perth: with all its complex history of interactions between First Nations and Migrant peoples.

The poems and stories in this collection range over a wide number of topics and themes: from a gruelling interrogation in Mongolia to the rapture of speaking in tongues. There is horseriding, choir-singing, and perfect *char bee hoon*. There is a mysterious child who can foretell disaster. There is grief: at the loss of a father, at the untimely death of a child; in lonely walks by the sea, and in empty nests. There is the bitterness of an incurable medical condition and the horror of the Plague Angel.

There is hope everywhere: unfurling like a question mark, blossoming like pea flowers, and in the legacy of a grandmother's prayer. There is love in a "coconut rough" voice and a lemon silk hat. There is a tribute to courage in the face of cancer. There is dancing around lines. There is a determined joy in birthday cakes. There is the wonder of a sneezing dragon.

We continue to thank the people who make *Seagift* possible: our family and friends, the staff and students of Sheridan, the Creative Writing Hub community, and the talented writers whose work is present in this collection. We are especially pleased to include some work from the Avondale University community in this issue.

We hope it brings you as much pleasure as it has brought us.

—Miriam Wei Wei Lo and Alison Dench

The Painting

MIKAYLA JOHNSON

The smell of paint filled my nose as the painting supplies were brought out. We were going to paint in class that day and everyone was buzzing with excitement. We were all told to put on our painting aprons, so we scrambled to get to where they were kept. I slid my uniform red apron over my shirt, bunching up the sleeves to free my hands.

Once I was assigned an easel, I stood in front of it. I stared at the large blank paper that was much bigger than my head and picked up a paintbrush. *What did I want to paint?*

I began with a sun. The kid next to me had painted a sun, so I figured it was a place to start. They had painted their sun in the other top corner though, so mine wasn't going to be the same. As I continued to put colour on the page, I suddenly had a great idea. I started to paint faster, with more passion. The smile on my face grew wider than before. Many colours started to blur together as I painted. My sun gained a green edge as I tried to paint the bright blue sky around it. After I had finished, I stood and admired my work.

The large, twisting, scaly, purple dragon stared at me, a look of betrayal on his face, as all around him were flowers: a vast field of flowers as far as the eye could see, flowers of many different shapes and colours. The dragon was allergic to flowers and pollen made him sneeze. He tried to stave off the inevitable with careful breaths and a claw under his nose. Alas, it was too late! He sneezed hard and fast, fire spewing out of his mouth and across the field, burning many flowers in its wake. The sun shone brightly in the corner of the canvas, suspended in a bright blue sky. I enthusiastically pointed out the details in my masterpiece. My teacher squinted at the seemingly random blobs of paint on the canvas, smiling and nodding as she wrote my intricate painting description in a small column down the side of the paper.

"What a wonderful story to go with your picture, Mikayla," she said as she wrote. "Be sure to share it with your Mum when she comes to pick you up today; I'm sure she'd love to hear it."

I grinned even wider as excitement filled me up. I knew Mum would love my masterpiece.

When I saw Mum that afternoon, I quickly jumped at the opportunity to tell her all about my painting and the dragon that was sneezing in the flower field. Mum thought my story was amazing and told me that she thought it was really cool. She was very interested in the painting and got me to point out the details as well as how the story was told in the picture. She smiled when she saw my teacher's description running down the side of the paper in a neat column and commented that mine was the only painting with such a long description of what it was.

Once we arrived at home, I showed it to Dad and my younger sister, Rachel. Dad exclaimed, "It looks great, sweety!" as he patted me on the shoulder. Both he and Rachel said it looked really cool.

That day, I felt like an artist, like I could do anything. I was filled with encouraging words and armed with an imagination. To others, that painting may just have been some blobs of paint on a canvas and not particularly impressive but, to me, it was my masterpiece.

Years later, I lean back in my desk chair, stretching out my arms. I smile as I look at the sketchbook that is laid out in front of me. The book is open to a freshly finished page. A sprawling fantasy map is spread across the paper with territories of different creatures marked with neat, dotted lines. There are mountain ranges, hilly areas, urbanised spaces, bridges, and coral reefs all marked with small symbols. Different biomes are indicated with coloured pencil shading: latitudinal lines helping to show general biome trends. I grin at my masterpiece, proud of how far I've come. I quickly take a photo to send to a few of my friends. As I await their replies, I gaze at my masterpiece.

It is not that painting of a sneezing dragon I made all those years ago, but the feeling in my chest is similar and, with it, there is a little nostalgia for the younger me. I plan to use this map to help me write a fantasy story but, for now, it's only a drawing: a drawing, and the ideas that are bubbling within my head. Over time, the masterpiece changes, but I hope I can always find that joy of creating something that I'm proud of.

Sweet Peas

CAROLYN RICKETT

for my parents

> *The green shoot will break through the rock …*
> *our tombs of loss will shatter, and there will be a*
> *homecoming. There will. There will. There will.*
> —Lewis Packer

Every year your hands wire trellis to the sloping fence
staking out the hope of something more than grey.

Then with a watering can you form a nimbus cloud
and rain on seeds in drought-bound soil.

We wait not knowing when the awkward stalk who keeps
tight-lipped for weeks might have something to say.

And always, every year, the first flower calls us outside
to hear its perfumed mouth finally speaking colour.

Thursday Night Dinner,
Dessert First

JUDITH HUANG

At the very heart of a Portuguese egg tart
is a gooey, sunshine-yellow custard
that spills out over your lip, warm and sweet
At the very heart of a ripe mango
is its sticky, orange centre
juices plosive with rounded tones
that enter your mouth's every corner
At the very heart of perfect *char bee hoon*
are the capable hands of my mother
dashing eggs against the wok
yellow and white, yellow and white
floofing up like a parachute
and blink-and-you-miss-it shakes of sugar
I am loved, I am loved
sings the very heart of it
And I listen with a very eager ear

Mill Town

AMANDA POPPE

Western Australia, 1902

He came to the West for a fresh start in a community that knew nothing of his past. He meant to work hard and get ahead and maybe, one day, to find a wife and raise a family. But the tiny mill town regarded Jim Crawley with suspicion. Tongues wagged and rumours flew and the little knots of people standing outside church stayed closed and hostile, so that he walked back to his makeshift tent and drowned his best intentions in beer.

When he came home from a long day of felling trees to find a wailing bundle outside his tent, the news flew around town faster than a buzz saw. The baby wasn't his. He knew it with a sad certainty, for he had not been with a woman for many years, but no one believed him. He went to every family begging them to take the infant, but they turned a cold shoulder.

"You've made your bed. Now sleep in it." And when they saw how beautiful the baby was, they added spitefully, "Leave it to die."

He couldn't do that.

"What will I feed her?" he cried as the last tin door slammed shut in his face. He slumped back to his tent and found a baby bottle and a supply of milk powder waiting for him. Somehow, he muddled through the feeding and the changing; and when he went back into the forest to fell the great Karri trees, the babe was strapped to his back, lulled to sleep by the rhythmic swinging of his axe.

She was an unusual child. Her eyes were so blue—strangely blue—and the wisps of hair so golden that he took to calling her 'Angel'. And perhaps an angel had come to live with him, for from the moment he found her outside his tent, things began to change for Jim. Or perhaps, with this little one depending on him, he worked harder and drank less and made more money, so that within a year of Angel's arrival, he had moved out of his tent and into a tin-roofed shack with wooden floors which he sanded to a fine smoothness so her little stumbling feet wouldn't get splinters. Of course, he couldn't take her with him into the forest anymore, so he paid Mrs. Larity to let the child run with her brood. And a rare, fast child she became.

She never complained, but only looked at you with those strange blue eyes that made you turn away. People in the mill town, especially those who said she should be left to die, could never quite meet her gaze. They would cross over to the other side when she came toddling down the street in her Sunday dress, holding Jim's finger in her pudgy fist.

By the time she could talk, they had more reason to be wary of her, for it became clear to everyone that she had a strange Gift.

She *knew* things.

The first time it happened, she was heading out with the Larity children for a swim but halfway down to the creek, she stood still and cried and refused to take another step. She was only two and could hardly talk, but she pulled on their skirts and hollered, "No swim! No swim!"

They got fed up with her and the oldest girl, Judith, carried her back to the house. But before they reached the veranda, the younger brother pounded up behind them, screaming at the top of his lungs. Half the town ran down to the creek and found the second boy, Andrew, floating face-down in the water.

People wondered, then, and whispered about it when they met in town. But how could a child of two know anything? And they shrugged it off.

A year later, the whole town was heading off to the bush for a day of picnicking and sport, and the mill boss arranged for the locomotive and carriage to take them all. Little Angel screamed and cried and wouldn't go on the train, so Jim had to take her home. Half an hour later he heard a terrible crash and, running down the line, he found the locomotive had gone off the rails and into the bush and the carriage had tipped. Amazingly, no one was hurt, but they all remembered how Angel had refused to get in the railcar.

From then on, they paid attention to what the little girl said and, for a long time, there were no disasters in the mill town and no funerals. People called her 'our guardian Angel', and they smiled at Jim and invited him over for dinner. On Saturday nights, when the town gathered at the store for euchre tournaments and dancing, Jim was in the middle of it all, his eyes bright with laughter as he swung Judith around on his arm until she begged to sit down her feet were so sore, and Angel crawled in her lap and fell asleep.

It would have gone on like that, presumably, for many happy years, except that one morning Jim was in a hurry to get to the mill. By this time, he was foreman and Angel, who was six, stood at the door.

She twisted her dress and said, "Daddy, I wish you wouldn't go to work today."

He kissed the top of her golden head and said, "Don't be silly, my Angel."

She had begun to feel self-conscious about her Gift, because the children at school teased her about it.

"You must be a witch. Your *mother* was a witch." And they shoved her in the dirt and said, "You're a Fallen Angel now."

So Angel didn't want to say anything to her father. She only said, "It's my birthday today."

Which it wasn't, Jim was going to point out, but then he realised it was the day she had appeared outside his tent all those years ago. And he said, "So it is, Angel. Your other birthday. We'll have to cook up something special for tea." And he gave her a coin and said, "Why don't you go to the store and buy yourself a treat."

She clung to his leg and said, "Can't you stay home today, Daddy?"

She whined so and it wasn't like her, and he was late and distracted because the big boss was coming that day and he had so many preparations to make. So he did something he had never done before—he smacked her on the bottom and said, "Now, girl, stop your whining." He felt bad, then, and added, "I'll make you a doll. Out of wood. I promise."

He hurried out of the house and didn't notice her following behind him, weeping and twisting her dress around her fingers.

Later that morning, as the great logs were rolling onto the conveyor belt, he heard a scream and looked up just in time to see a log tumbling toward him. He jammed his pole into the ground and leapt out of the way. The log hit the pole and twisted sideways. He saw a flash of golden hair and blue, blue eyes looking up at him; and then she was gone, crushed under the weight of the log.

And when they got it off her, he held her broken body in his arms and wept. "She tried to tell me. She tried to tell me … ."

The whole town came out for the funeral, so that they jammed the little church full and craned their necks around the doorway. Many hands reached out to touch the tiny coffin on the way to the cemetery under the peppermint trees. The Larity children gathered in close, and Judith slipped her hand in his as the box was laid in the ground.

A cloud hung over the town because their Angel had gone home, and the mill stood silent for many days. But the felling and hauling and cutting and sawing had to go on, and when Jim failed to show up for work, the boss put someone else in his place.

Judith brought a dish of hot food over to Jim's house but when she pushed open the door, he wasn't there. She set the food down on the dirty counter and hurried to the peppermint grove where she found him slumped amidst the graves and a scattering of beer bottles.

She touched him, and he didn't move. She shook him fearfully. He rolled over and gazed up at her stupidly. In a burst of anger she cried, "Did her life mean nothing to you?" She picked up a bottle and threw it hard so that it shattered against a tree trunk then ran away, sobbing.

Jim called out and staggered after her as far as the peppermint tree. He stared down at the broken glass until the pieces blurred and melted in his tears.

When the light was fading and the kookaburras were laughing, he knelt beside the freshly scraped earth and whispered, "I'm listening now. I'm listening."

The next day he reported to work, but the boss took one look at his bloodshot eyes and told him he could clean up the yard. Which Jim did all the long hot day. And the next. And the next.

Every evening, he walked down to the peppermint grove and didn't come home till after dark. One day Judith followed him, her heart heavy, and found him sitting on a rock beside Angel's grave, carving a piece of wood. She leaned against the tree and watched the shavings fall to the ground and, after a long silence, Jim started to talk. The words tumbled out like wood chips falling, shaping the memories and the questions that had no answers. Judith hugged her knees and listened. Sometimes the pain made them cry and sometimes it made them laugh but, when the light was almost gone, Jim set the wooden doll on the grave, took Judith's hand in his, and together they walked back to town.

It wasn't long before Jim got his job back and, soon after that, the whole town gathered again at the church, this time for a wedding. Jim took Judith to live in the big manager's house and, over the years, they filled the rooms with running, laughing children. When the day's work was done, the family would gather on the veranda in summer or around the woodstove in winter. Jim would sit in the comfy chair with a child or two on his lap and the rest at his feet, and he would tell stories of his childhood out east and of his work as a lumberjack. When he tried to send them off to bed, they'd cry, "Just one more, Daddy. You haven't told us our *favourite*."

And then he'd kiss their bright faces and hug them close and tell them about the angel who came to town and chose to live with him.

It Shouldn't Be Allowed

ANGELINE YAP

It cannot be right
that the coffin's so tiny.
There ought to be a rule.

... and when at night you close your eyes,
behind your eyelids, she is still alive,

she laughs and plays and calls to you,
her little fingers take hold of your hand.

It just can't be correct
that the coffin's so tiny.
It shouldn't be allowed.

These Papers

ANDREW LANSDOWN

for my father

All these papers he put his life into—
sermon manuscripts and lecture outlines,
Bible study notes and children's talks,
meeting minutes and diary entries ...
No one wants them, all these papers,
not even his last living son. For

what can I do with them all? When
would I ever get time even to read them?
I have mounds of my own writings—
essays and sermons, poems and stories—
to deal with, and more on the way,
more with more things I want to say.

I know, with something of the feeling
of my father's feeling, that come my time
to leave my home for a "home",
my children, too, without malice
and maybe with a little sadness,
will likely compost the leaves of my life.

Instead of working at these pages,
I sometimes think I might as well
have grubbed the soft fern shoots
to stave my hunger, like the bowmen of Shu.
Sometimes like them I wonder
who can know our sorrow, who?

Endnote:
See Ezra Pound's translation of an early Chinese poem "Song of the
Bowmen of Shu"

The Interrogation

ALISON DENCH

Moon faced and magnificent, Ariuka *Bagsh* beams across the professionally laminated vowel chart that straddles both her desk and mine. She's rather upbeat. Instructing me in basic Mongolian fortuitously supplements her teaching of Russian in a local high school. But the academic year is done, and her regular students have evaporated under summer sunshine. Now, it's just me and the vowels: seven solo structures and twelve muscular clusters, formidable and foreboding, like an encampment of *Chinggis Khan*'s army.

A week earlier, I arrowed into the nation's capital, Ulan Bator, through a slim window of tranquillity. There was time enough to stock up on hard-to-get supplies. Within days the weather worsened; the airport shut; and my American team leaders and I struggled for more than three hours, heading north to my new home, a community close to the Russian border. At times, the Landcruiser was almost airborne, locked in a non-stop, apocalyptic dust storm. Nothing of what *Lonely Planet* (the go-to travel guide) promised—verdant pastureland, cascades of lowing cattle, and huddles of felt tents—was visible. Just dust.

Language school stands out: a strip of blue zinc on a blistering face of grey. It's a brightly painted, converted ground-level apartment within a huge five-storey block. The massive concrete complex, built in the 1960s under Russian rule, is home to hundreds of families. Alongside the school, a cobalt blue iron door shuts out street life and leads into a dark, littered foyer, the base of the first flight of stairs and the location of two apartment doors. Our classrooms, though, have direct street access via three long cement steps, chipped and stained, spilling onto the dirt road. The school's only front window is ensconced in a web of twisted steel, decorative protection against crime.

It's now June 2008 and—armed only with a bi-lingual dictionary, the spectacular vowel chart, and the introductory booklet—I have completed my twelve-day-long Survival Course. I'm not sure anything has stuck. None of the teachers speak English. I don't speak Mongolian apart from some 'shopping phrases' and a few newly acquired guttural sounds that are absent from English phonology. There are no grammar notes in English, and I'm scrabbling to decipher the Russian Cyrillic alphabet—into which Mongolia's ancient, curling, vertical script has been horizontally transliterated. Unbelievably, there is a test: seven written questions and an oral examination which I need to pass to advance.

Ariuka *Bagsh*, despite her competence, is under orders. The Director of the Language School, Mönkh *Darak*, who has permeated each day's lesson via the chic 'click clicking' of her stilettos nearby, has decided to personally conduct the oral assessment. Short, rotund, and brusque, she batters her way through impossibilities. She gives the impression she could run a small country from her shower cubicle. I can only think of daleks and wonder whether I'll be exterminated!

It's time. I'm summoned to her office. With sundry greetings aside, and replicating one of the Survival Course scenarios, Mönkh *Darak* expertly introduces the subject of purchasing. Diving into a heaped corner of the room, she produces Exhibit A: a glamorous handbag. Then, in stilted Mongolian, as if dialling down the speed settings on a YouTube video, she very deliberately declares: "I ... bought ... this." Quite wondrously, I cotton on. It's the perfect opportunity to practise my interrogatives.

"When?" I ask. Mönkh *Darak*'s eyes brighten.

"Yesterday." The conversation picks up.

"Where?" I continue.

"At the markets," she enthusiastically responds.

I'm on a roll. My inner linguist fires up, trawling for more Mongolian question words. Within seconds, the inevitable spills out of my mouth: "How much?" Mönkh *Darak* stops abruptly, raises a well-groomed eyebrow, and considers. A rush of heat scorches upward and my face colours crimson. *Oh no!* I think. *Am I dead meat? Is it culturally inappropriate to ask a person what they've spent?* My heart tries to escape through the roof of my mouth.

I remember the first day I entered this office, a fortnight ago. A co-worker had introduced me to Mönkh *Darak*, and they had collegially agreed on the terms and conditions of my language study. Laughing and joking, my South African teammate had swung her huge arms around the room, in all-encompassing arcs, summarising the mood with the simple Mongolian phrase *ger bül*: family. I wonder if I'm still considered part of the family. *What shame have I brought on my organisation? Have I committed an unforgiveable offence, questioning the Director's buying habits? I'm supposed to be on this student visa for a full two years, but she could quickly put a stop to that.* Normally articulate, I realise I don't have the words to extricate myself.

Mönkh *Darak* smiles thinly and gives a quick nod of approval. She utters a number. It sounds like a lot of money, but I'm not entirely sure it is. My grasp of Mongolian numerals is still quite rudimentary.

"*Ünetei*," I proclaim. It seems like the right thing to say and, besides, the word 'expensive' is on my vocabulary list. A moment of silence hangs dangerously. And then, leaning the full weight of her body on the adjectival modifier, Mönkh *Darak* loudly exclaims: "*A-i-m-a-a-r ... ünetei*!"

With that, the oral assessment is over. It seems to have gone well. She has withstood my barrage of pointed questions, showcasing authoritative opulence. I have survived, exhausting the arsenal of my known vocabulary. A strange warmth piles up between us. It's enough to sustain us through a snowy autumn and one of the coldest winters on record.

Note: Names have been changed to protect identities.

Glossary:

Bagsh: Teacher
Chinggis Khan: Genghis Khan
Darak: Director/Head
ünetei: expensive
aimaar ünetei: terrifyingly expensive

Come Upon Me

SAMUEL MITCHELL

This is a sign,
this rush of words
—lush linguistic flow—
tongue and lips, teeth and gums,
cheeks and jaw bones loosed
from grinding inefficiency
by the oil of Your presence.
Come upon me.
Dwell within me.
Can this stinking shell
be a holy fane?
Can this cobwebbed mind comprehend You
and still remain sane?
remain the same?
You are not an Energy
(pure or otherwise).
Not some shampoo-smelling cloud of amorality,
showering salubrious goodness
upon both the tyrants and the self-sacrificing
of this   wor
bro ke   l
     n   d.

No.
Please give me your wine.
(Heady, crushing, cleansing.)
Your blood is smeared
upon the doorposts of my heart—
it is Your mark.
Be in me the lighted candle
that defies the advancing dark.

Poet of Jazz

STEPHANIE DENNIS

For my husband Jake

He croons Natalie Cole's "Inseparable",
his voice coconut rough
as I wait side stage holding Jiminy Cricket
to help us wish upon a star.

He is the only man I know
who moves with flair like Fred Astaire
until Alzheimer's silent seniors sing along.
I pour bourbon on the rocks

for my milky choc gentleman.
Swallowtails in my stomach.
He kisses my forehead, his fingers
brown paws on my cheeks.

What a man! Performer *and* poet!
Winter midnights: his Hercules hands tenderly glide
down my arm, burst strawberries in my mouth
as we soak in bubble-gum bath bubbles;

his hint to claim, "you're mine."
At Joe's Fish Shack we dined, drank Majella's
The Musician wine, turning me gazelle shy
with his dazzling Burmese brown eyes.

I've been waiting... all my life, for you.

You gave me my first *sakura* tea ceremony,
olive pickling, Swan grape picking,
trip to Perth Zoo, escargot, *agedashi* tofu,
me singing "Music Box" in Ngilgi Cave to you.

I've always known the stars... made you, for me.

Where others saw a rat's tail, bat
fangs, cat claws, I saw the Lion King
of my heartbeat, beating like a gorilla
on African drums; my cute penguin.

On his feet, in his arms for eternity and beyond
blissfully dancing on the lyrics of songs,
"together, wherever we go!" Forever,
the ink of our love poems in our hearts overflow.

Flatwork in the Present

JACKSON BLACK

The train rattles and clatters, swaying from side to side ever so slightly. If it weren't for the houses whipping past outside the window, it could be mistaken for a ponderous beast of burden, like a camel reluctantly carrying its cargo of commuters to a far-off place. Through the window, the sky above the hills is a deep blue, tinted with pink. It's ten to five on a July evening. Soon the sun will flee out past the sea, completely abandoning the hills to the grey of winter twilight. Unlike the other commuters, I vacantly gaze out the window, phone in my pocket, backpack beneath my crossed legs. The day is nearly done, nothing more to do. No more customers, managers, procedures, or things to learn. I can just relax. The train lurches, rolling homeward as the shadows chase after the sun. After an age of blurred rooftops, the train slides into the station. The brakes let out a soft moan and a few overly eager passengers, who've stood up, lean sharply into the deceleration.

"Doors opening," states the automated voice. With a click, they slide back. The cool chill of winter air fills the carriage as the warm mass of passengers leaves it. I stand, fumbling for my keys in the pockets of my pants. My backpack dangles by a strap from one hand as I flounder my way out of the carriage, trying to disentangle the keys while watching where I'm going. It takes me several moments to refocus on where I am and step out the door of the train. Finally, my keyring loosens its grasp on the corner of my wallet, though by now most of the other passengers have already left. The station is nearly empty aside from a pair of train guards watching disinterestedly. Maybe, they're at the end of their shift? Standing in their short-sleeved shirts with their arms crossed, they certainly look like they'd rather be done for the day. I totter up the steep stairs of the bridge leading out of the train station, huddling into my jacket. Once I'm in the car, it'll be warmer.

As I pull into the driveway, I can see the sun hovering over the horizon, ready to make its final dash. By now the sky has turned a plum blue, less pink-tinged than purple. The windows at the front of the house gleam with yellow light. Mum's leaning over her laptop in her office. Her elbows are on the desktop. As she's staring intently at her screen, battering away at the keyboard, I can tell she's found a rare moment to focus and get stuff done. Meanwhile, Hazel teeters on the arm of the couch next to the loungeroom window, practically bouncing on her little Jack-Russell tail as she watches me clamber from the car. With a clatter, I unlatch the door, and the scraping click of her sliding and scrambling across the tiles of the entry hall declares her thrill at seeing someone arrive home.

"Hey, how are you going?" says Mum.

"Fine. Big day." I respond.

"You didn't message me when you left work. Are you riding tonight?"

I look up from unlacing my shoes and fending off the canine bundle of anarchy trying to climb onto my lap. I'd forgotten in the rush of the day that I needed to ride tonight. *How could I forget? There'd be no other time this week if I wanted to ride; my evenings are all full.*

It's too cold, though.

Without meaning to, I sigh.

"I should."

"Tonight's the only chance you have till the weekend."

"I'm tired."

Mum glances at me over her reading glasses. The dog bounces around my feet.

"If you'd let me know you were on your way, I could have tacked Astro up for you."

"I forgot."

"Well, you can't ride now. You won't have much light left by the time you tack up."

There's a moment of silence after she says this, watching me over her glasses. *I wish she wouldn't stare at me. Especially after a day at work when I just want to rest. Should I be responsible? The last thing I want to do right now is ride. It'd mean getting Astro out of the paddock, brushing him down, tacking him up, riding in the cold.*

"I know. I'll go get sorted."

I wander off to my room to get changed out of my work clothes and into my breeches. *Horses. Whatever possessed me to ride horses?*

By the time I've changed and unpacked, Mum has moved to the kitchen to start prepping for dinner. Dad will be back from work soon and the sounds of the rest of the family finishing their day fill the house. Outside, the light has begun to fade to the grey haze of twilight, but the house is lit with a soft golden glow. It's warm, slightly noisy, homely. And I'm going to go ride.

As I walk past the kitchen, I hear Mum call out.

"What was that?" I call back, not stopping walking.

"I said that you took a long time getting changed," she responds.

I shake my head and keep walking.

Outside, the wind has picked up. It's now no longer a slight breeze but instead steadily blowing: not enough to be a proper gust but enough to drag the cold air down from the hills.

In the paddocks, the horses are waiting at the gates. They know its nearly dinner time, and Sox, Paddy, and Boo all prick up their ears. Astro also pricks his ears in his paddock, though he hangs back from the gate, giving Missy space as she leans over the white-painted fence rail. He may be a massive Hanoverian, but he's not about to get in the way of the bossy little station-mare when she's waiting for food. She's top of the pecking order; everyone knows it. As I walk across the yard,

Sox lets out a whinny and Paddy stamps. Missy joins in. Astro, however, just snorts and lowers his head to the ground, watching me patiently as if to say, "You just take your time; it's a bit late for riding but not for dinner."

"You and me both, mate," I mumble as I grab his halter from the hook beside the gate. I squeeze under the top rail, stepping around Missy. Astro doesn't lift his head as I approach.

"Come here, mate. We're going for a ride." I sling the lead rope around his neck, then ram the stiff throat-lash through the buckle of his halter. He slowly meanders along behind me as I push Missy away from the gate and fumble with the clasp. A moment later, a soft, large muzzle slides into the corner of my eye and against my face, before Astro rests his head on my shoulder.

"Oi," I deftly sidestep. His head is as big as my upper body. In fact, his head probably weighs more than my upper body. "You're too big!"

Astro watches me with one of his brown eyes. He nuzzles at my shoulder again, not leaning quite so much on me this time. He wants attention and care rather than just be left to his own devices. In a way, that makes me feel a little happier and a little less wired. It's all so simple. Not a care in the world except for being cared for. A focus on the present rather than the past or the future. I smile, despite the gate latch that really shouldn't be as stuck as it is.

"Come on, then."

The gate comes free. As we walk up to the stables, Astro stays right by my side. I lead him into the cross-ties, tapping his shoulder to get him to spin around, so he's facing toward me. There's a soft scraping sound as his hindquarters rub across the brick of the stable wall and his chest rubs across the wooden railing on the other side. The tie-up bay is built for a normal-sized horse. With a click, I attach the two ties to Astro's halter, stopping him from wandering away while I pull his mud-caked rug off. Thanks to the rug and the clear, rainless day, his fluffy winter coat is mostly clean.

After a quick brush, I grab my tack out, first throwing a saddle pad on and then my dressage saddle, doing up the girth tightly to hold everything in place. Astro drops his head so I can put his bridle on. If he wasn't so obliging, most people would be unable to put the headpiece over his ears without a stepladder. I check the buckles and straps one last time. Once, tacking-up would have taken me half an hour. Now, it takes me ten minutes. Even so, the sky is darkening, plum fading to black.

Out in the arena-paddock, I lead Astro over to an old stump, so I can swing myself up into the saddle. He stands, his ears swivelling back to listen to me, then darting back around to listen to other noises. With a soft click of my tongue and a gentle push with my legs, I ask him to walk.

The bottlebrushes that line the arena sway gently in the wind, as first we warm up at a walk, then transition to a trot. I pulse my ring fingers on the reins and half halt with my seat, driving him forward with my legs while at the same time asking him to lift his back. Together we steady ourselves, not speeding up. The goal is to make him take longer, more powerful steps, to carry himself in a good posture that develops muscle, flexibility, balance, and strength. Half-halting with my seat, using the muscles in my core, helps us.

Up, down, up down, left right, left right, up down, up down—we trot a circle across the sand of the arena. Astro is listening, focusing, ignoring the evening sounds now. His ears stay pinned to the front, only swivelling when I make a noise or give a command with my seat. *Where are my hands? Am I carrying them in front of myself like I'm holding a tray? Or have I once more dropped them down toward my legs? Am I keeping them still while my elbows and shoulders absorb the movement and cadence of Astro's paces? Can I feel his hind legs pistoning forward underneath me, connecting with the ground where his front legs were only moments before, then pushing, launching into the next step?*

These thoughts all whirl through my mind. We work through trot and canter, loops and circles, across the diagonal of the arena. We try to lengthen and shorten our strides, taking bigger or shorter steps without changing their speed. Astro shortens beautifully, but every time I squeeze with my leg to ask him to lengthen, the thummp thummp thummp of our steady trot breaks into a thumpthumpthump of fast, short steps. The trot gets messy and uneven. Unbalanced. Yet after a while we get a lengthen that is passable, though not good. Enough of a success that we can refocus onto something else.

We move to laterals, shoulder-ins and leg-yields, where we incorporate sideways movement. Each shift sideways is an extra requirement for coordination on my behalf, adding new complications. Astro listens to every aid I use, both good and bad. When I lift my hand, loosening the rein, he surges forward. When I drop my hand, unintentionally blocking, he stops going forwards. When everything is where it should, we settle into a balanced rhythm.

Despite everything that needs to be refined and corrected, we glide across the sand getting smoother, more coordinated with each movement. It almost feels like floating. The sun finally makes its escape over the horizon. The moon balances atop the hills above, proclaiming its victory to the stars. It is rich and rotund, gleaming like mercury. The sand of the arena glows a soft white-grey in its light. The shadowed gums and bottlebrushes are darker, with silver-filigreed leaves flickering in the wind. Finally, once the last of the sunlight is gone, I drop the reins. Astro settles into a steady walk as I wrap my arms around his sweaty, fluffy, warm neck.

"You're such a good boy. Thank you."

He stops and turns his head back to look at me. Then he shakes and nods toward the stables.

"Yes, its dinner time, mate. You're such a good boy."

My voice is perhaps a little singsong, like an older brother doting on their much younger baby sibling. I flick a leg over his back and drop to the ground, gathering my reins. We march back toward the stables. I untack Astro, brushing him down with a coarse brush, taming fluff and removing sweat and sand. He rumbles, nudging at my pockets.

"Be patient!"

Later that night, as I step back into the warm glow of the house after feeding Astro, Mum calls from the kitchen.

"Are you feeling better, grump?"

There's a teasing hint of 'I told you so' in her voice.

I smile, lean against the wall, and pull my boots off. We both know the answer to her question.

"Just a little."

Horses. Thank God for horses.

Line

ARIEL JUNE CHEN

Lines to make.
Lines to keep.
Lines to blur.
Lines to cross.

    Make a line, please.
    Keep to the line, please.
    Don't blur the line, please.
    Don't cross the line, please.

        Can you cross over the line?
        Tell me, where is the line?
        Tell me, am I out of line?
        Step over the line.

            Cross the line for me.
            Blur the line with me.
            The lines are killing me.
            Ignore the line with me.

                Dance around the line with me.

Adjustment

NATALIE CHER LEITÃO

I am struggling with the fit of this new coat
like a small child within whom there is promise
of longer limbs,
a taller torso,
a stronger body that will (one day)
wear the garment with confidence.
But for now, the coat is at least three sizes too big.
And at times it is
suffocating me.

I catch my breath as I pass his bedroom.
Ten months ago, it overflowed with sport shoes, uni files, and
Lynx body spray aromas.
Now, the room is an empty shell.

My footsteps echo as I collect discarded items:
a shirt (too small),
a pair of socks (too stretched),
and sunglasses (too scratched).
There's an old hair clipper set,
strands of black hair still caught between metal teeth.
There's the custom wrap spray paint he used on his car,

the car he exchanged for an
engagement ring.

I place them all in an empty wash basket.
I recall the days this basket held freshly washed nappies.
Then school uniforms.
Then men's trousers and shirts which hung
on the Hills Hoist and somehow dwarfed
his father's clothing.
Our son is now a man.
A husband.

On his wedding day, I watched him watching
his bride enter the church.
His bottom lip quivered
as did
mine.
I couldn't be prouder,
and yet
I am struggling
with the fit
of this
new
coat.

A Thousand Tangled Threads

ZOE COCHRANE

The old church loomed above the suburban streets of Blacktown, casting a mishappen shadow over the footpath below. It was no stone beauty with its extensive history mapped out in Gothic columns like the churches of her homeland, but the familiar tones of the pipe organ which spilled out onto the street began to soothe the fear which rooted her to the sidewalk.

The entrance was so close, and the suit-clad greeter had been glaring at her loitering for some time, but to move was a monumental task.

It had been many years since Ingrid Meijer had entered a church. Her faith was as strong as ever, but in her mind the image of a church would be forever bathed in crimson swastikas.

"Moeder, are we ever going inside?" Rheene, her eldest, muttered impatiently. "We're going to be late!"

Her youngest, Erik, was not as quick to voice impatience as his sister, but his longing gaze was fixed on a group of young boys who were giving the greeter increasingly enthusiastic handshakes.

Remember, Ingrid, you are doing this for their sake.

"Ja," she stated determinedly, "let us go in."

As she climbed the stone steps, she locked eyes with the greeter once more and hoped it was her nerves which caused her to see disgust blooming in his beady eyes. Plastering on her best smile, she stuck out her gloved hand expectantly.

"Happy Sabbath," she chirped. "We are new here and have only ever experienced worship in a small house church. I hear you have a children's class; can you help me find it?"

At the word 'new' his eyes narrowed to harsh points, and he waved a dismissive hand towards a long hallway beyond, "Out the back, there's a shed."

Smiling to hide the fact she knew not what a 'shed' might be, she herded her children inside the hall, chose a direction, and prayed she was correct. Pacing determinedly, she felt Rheene lightly tug her in the direction of a non-descript door. Sure enough, another mother swung it open, and the sound of squealing children wafted out.

"Will you be okay, Moeder?" Erik whispered as they approached the courtyard.

Ingrid's heart was warmed by his care, but she resolved to do a better job of hiding her fear. She would not taint this experience for her children.

"Ja, Erik," she assured. "Rheene, when class is over, I want you and your brother to be inside the church before the main bell. Do you understand?"

"Ja, Moeder," Rheene sing-songed before dashing away in a twirl of rose skirts to join the children throwing a ball. Erik, not one to be left behind, quickly followed, leaving Ingrid alone once more.

With no one fuelling her determination, Ingrid felt the familiar nerves creep in, trying to convince her that the black suits of the men were uniforms and the brown carpets stained with blood. The first mournful notes of the organ starting up again tore her from her haze, and she hurried to join the line of men and women waiting to enter the main church.

Smoothing the wrinkles out of her lilac skirt, she waited tensely until the line shuffled forth enough for her to spy an empty seat at the back and slide into it with a relieved sigh. There would be time before the head elder opened the class and she examined the space around her. The style was ... unfortunate, but then Adventists were notorious for choosing function and frugality over 'senseless frivolity'. If all went well today, then this would be her first proper church, these outdated orange walls and home-made scripture tapestries would be the monikers of home, and these people seated in the miles of pews before her would be her second family.

Even in her own mind it sounded too optimistic.

The longer she waited, the more a strange prickling sensation seemed to wash over her skin. Covertly, she shifted her gaze and spotted two women in feathered, red hats staring openly at her from a neighbouring pew, muttering angrily under their breath. They were not alone. The gaze of the three elders on stage was a disapproving weight, and more in the crowd were catching on.

A strange numbness arose as more caught on to the staring and began casting her glances also. She could not fathom what she had done, but Ingrid felt the sharpness of those eyes and the all-consuming numbness root her to her seat.

Even as the head elder shuffled his ancient bones to the pulpit, the whispers continued; and Ingrid forced herself to look attentive, flicking the pages of her Bible, saying quiet "amens" in all the right places, all the while sucking in shallow breaths and praying she'd last the class.

As the soprano screeched the final torturous note of the closing hymn, Ingrid stumbled upright and dashed for the hall stairs leading to the basement. No matter what lay beneath the building, she would find sanctuary there for a few precious moments. With each descending step, she felt her breath quickening in her chest as panic threatened to destroy her careful façade. The sound of women's laughter behind her had Ingrid hurrying as fast as she dared in heels, unwilling to let them see her cry.

Past what appeared to be bathrooms lay an inconspicuous oak door and she clumsily shoved it open, getting a vague image of box towers through watery eyes before she was whirling around to shut the door. Squeezing her eyes tightly shut, Ingrid rested her forehead against the steady surface with a shaky sigh.

How fast I've forgotten what it feels like to be watched ...

"If you're gonna stand there and cry you can find some other place, reffo."

The rough voice shattered Ingrid's sanctuary and, with a barely stifled shriek, she whirled to face the room, her bluebell gaze locking almost immediately with sharp hazel barely two metres away.

At the sight of her shock, the stranger scoffed, her dark eyes narrowing pensively.

"You should check ya hideouts more thoroughly."

Strangely, despite the emotional turmoil of the day and her usual meekness, the woman's sarcastic tone sent a thrill of anger zinging through her blood.

"I am not crying."

Most women from her homeland would scamper away from such a sharp tone, but the stranger let loose a deep, barking laugh, her ebony curls jiggling in time.

"Finally," she drawled, "it talks. Word of advice, reffo, crying will get ya nowhere 'round here."

Stupidly, though she knew she'd done no wrong, Ingrid felt compelled by the woman's no-nonsense tone to explain herself. To find some sympathy in this heartless woman.

"I did nothing wrong; I do not understand why they stare."

The woman's square features sharpened in a scowl.

"Ya seriously don't know?"

Ingrid's confused expression said it all, and the woman was soon releasing another barking laugh tinged with bitterness.

"It's ya hat and ya husband."

Shock hit her like a punch in the gut. "What?" Ingrid hissed, "I don't understand."

"They're upset," the stranger drawled, "because ya have the audacity to come to church without a hat and a husband. They think you're an upstart immigrant."

The husband she could understand, but a hat? Blinking slowly, Ingrid thought back to the hazy memories of her childhood home-church, and her heart sunk as she recalled her naïve curiosity at the extravagant velvet hats the adults had worn despite their humble surroundings. Memory had been her companion for so long, how could it have failed her today?

"Oh," she heard herself whisper, numbly.

"Yeah, it's a bloody stupid tradition, but tradition none the less."

With a sudden cracking of stiff knees and a flurry of flowered fabric, the stranger stood and ambled towards Ingrid, an indifferent expression perched on her cherry lips. Ingrid watched, dumbly, as the woman thrust out a gloved hand and brandished a lemon silk hat that was only slightly dented at the back.

"It was the best I could do in an hour," she muttered nonchalantly. "Don't forget next week."

Ingrid tentatively plucked up the hat and set it atop her pale curls. It fit perfectly. Numb from the emotions of the day, she visualised this stranger spending an hour painstakingly sewing daisies onto its smooth surface and found her heart blooming hope anew at the simple kindness of this rough Australian.

"Thank you," she whispered.

The woman cleared her throat loudly and made to exit the room, pausing only momentarily to throw over her shoulder, "The name is Nancy Mackintosh, and if ya want things to change, think about what I've said."

In a flurry of voluminous skirts, she was gone.

***

Nancy's parting words plagued Ingrid's mind throughout the main service and, between her musings and ensuring her children behaved, she had little time to focus on the stares boring into her spine.

By the time the benediction was uttered and the crowd ambled out to the courtyard for a 'pot-luck' lunch, Ingrid found resolution bolstering her courage. She did want things to change.

Marrying Kristopher, a relative stranger, and taking the family on the first passage to Australia had been part youthful exuberance and part necessity. There was little left of the Netherlands once the bombs had done their work. But the 'golden country' of the papers was proving a tougher place than she expected.

While unsympathetic, Nancy's words had taught her one thing: There was no use crying over her troubles when there was still a life to be had.

"Oi, reffo, you're blocking the beans!"

Torn from her thoughts, Ingrid found she was indeed blocking the green beans and, directing a sheepish smile at those around her, she murmured a quick, "My apologies," and stepped neatly aside.

Her hopes of avoiding conflict were dashed when the same nasally voice from before muttered in a falsetto mimicry, "My apologies," before letting out a full-bellied guffaw. Casting a disapproving eye at the perpetrator, Ingrid was unsurprised to see it was the greeter who had been glaring at her since the moment she arrived.

Unnerved by the mockery, Rheene's loose grip on her skirts tightened and she cast her mother a look of worry. Quickly, Ingrid steadied her plate and made to leave the greeter to his own detestable jokes, before another man, emboldened by his friend's display, called after her, "Oi, Nazi, what right do you have to act so high and mighty?"

The background chatter died away at the cruel taunt and Ingrid could feel those awful eyes boring into her skin once more. But in that moment, with anger slowly blooming in her heart, Ingrid could not care less.

"What did you call me?"

The pair leered at her, proud they'd struck a nerve. "You heard me, Nazi."

Ingrid knew she should walk away and avoid further conflict. This morning she wouldn't have hesitated. It wasn't ladylike to argue so publicly. But while she had had much practice turning her cheek, there were some things she simply couldn't forgive.

"What's wrong? Your ears painted on, Nazi?" the greeter baited.

Flashes of memory flowed like water through her mind. Huddling behind her mother's skirts as tanks rolled down main street. Mechanically chewing through stewed tulip bulbs when the supply chains were stopped. Covering her ears from whistling bombs. Clinging desperately to her sister's cold, skeletal form.

Indignation that these ignorant beasts would dare mistake her for such people burnt through any remaining nerves and, taking a deep breath, she stared them straight in the eye.

"I have never been, nor will I ever be a Nazi! I know you people detest being flooded with immigrants, and that you fear what it will mean. I'm sorry, I truly am, but whether you like it or not I believe that anyone who calls themselves a Christ-like individual should at least have the brains to look past one's accent."

For a moment there was silence, and Ingrid steeled herself to leave if the confrontation grew uglier, but Nancy's familiar voice soon cut through the tension with a sarcastic snort.

"Ha! Jerry, I knew ya dropped outta school, but I figured you could at least tell a Dutch woman from a German one!"

One by one the stony faces around her melted with bellows of laughter and the two perpetrators ducked their heads with flaming cheeks. Ingrid swept the sea until she spotted Nancy's smug grin across the way. Locking gazes, Ingrid's heart bloomed with pride at the Australian's simple nod.

Maybe change isn't so hard after all.

***

The shadow of the old church had spread, blanketing the street in darkness by the time Ingrid was allowed to leave. After her altercation, Nancy had taken the opportunity to introduce Ingrid to her friends. One blur of faces and names later, Ingrid had spent the afternoon swapping household tips and commiserating over lazy husbands before walking away with several offers for tea.

By the exhausted smiles painted on her children's faces, they had experienced similar success.

"Will we come again next week, Moeder?" Erik murmured hopefully, gazing back at the other families.

Ingrid paused at the bottom of the stone steps and followed his gaze. In the blood-red sunset the church's dilapidated form no longer seemed so terrible. For the first time in twenty years, the threads of her life didn't seem so tangled, and she looked at worn stone steps without seeing her father's blood or hearing his echoed screams on the wind. Instead, the gentle melody of the organist seemed to whisper an invitation.

Come, you are welcome here.

"Ja, Erik. I think we will."

The Kingdom of Heaven

MIRIAM WEI WEI LO

(Matthew 5 & 13)

It could
be like this:
the tiny seed stuck
like a burr in the mind:
annoying, prickly,
unshakeable;

its head
a leaf raises   like a question
finding cracks;   that we'd prefer
built for   to ignore,
questing root,   then another,
that first   another, until they are
sending out   waving at us, so many
slowly swelling   frantic green hands;
^   and the roots,
so slender at first,
barely noticeable,
have grown
as thick as legs
that can squeeze
rocks apart;
and we find
we are able
to love
our enemies
and sit down
to eat
with them;

who's right
and who's wrong:
forgotten, crushed into dust
beneath our feet
as we feast
together.

Creature Discomforts

BEN LEE

Corin, so glad I've found you at last. What have they done to you? You're so small, your scales dulled. Well. I've brought flowers—tulips, red riding hoods. Lovely, aren't they? My first successful ones, lovely striped leaves. I hope you feel alright about that; *Gracie, do you honestly think I look like I'm one for roses?* is what you used to say, before the change. I think flowers can brighten the soul of any boy or girl, man or … monster. There, I said it. Sorry. I've opened the windows a little for a bit of breeze. The staff here are fine. I've wiped their minds; they're sleeping downstairs. I can't believe this—no views, no air, barely any food or water—it's like they want you to die, and faster. Well, not here, not now. I'm here to take you home, to set you free.

I hope you won't be upset. You said, before you became like this, that you never wanted to live a day longer than you had a right to, and I've wanted to respect that; but till God tells me otherwise, I can't let you die here, certainly not like this. I've always thought you were meant for more. Besides, things out there have changed. What with the world forgetting you, and Dad gone—well, there's just no one left anymore who used to bother you. You seem very still, Corin. I hope I haven't offended you. Or maybe it's shock? The good kind, maybe?

We're going back to the Manor—yes, our little hut on the top of the hill we called the Manor that was always ours, inherited from Nan, and Mum—a few renovations made there in light of your condition, nothing more. Corin, please don't be mad at me. I hope the silence is a kind of expectation? I've found it hard to read you, especially since, well, you know. You lost your speaking voice. Grew those scales, horns, and claws. And that hair, almost a beast in itself, would rival a crocodile for length. Dad was intolerably cruel, he was—first the curse of calling you a monster, me a freak, then leaving us out of the will. But don't you worry about him anymore. However you feel about him, he's in God's hands now. For the sake of your soul, you'd do well to let him out of yours. Forgive him, Corin.

It's time to make sure our hearts are right, Corin. I'm so glad I've found you now and not a moment later. They reckon the death will come in six weeks; it's not simply neglect that the asylum's been skint on food lately. The country's dying faster than we can believe. Has anyone told you about the Plague Angel? We don't know much about it. Some sort of being sucking the life out of Perth, now making its way through all the other states like a bushfire. See, this isn't the way to go—if there's only weeks or days left, I want to spend them together with you.

***

You're starting to grow already, and you've only had lunch. Don't worry about the room. I don't care that you've clawed chunks out of the walls or that the chair with the wonky leg is bent to the shape of your grip. Under the circumstances, what is the point of a heritage listing? Your rages are a part of you and you can't control them, not once they're in motion. And my arm, it's nothing a bandage won't fix (thanks, Kevin). It's time to put things right now we're finally at the Manor. I'll leave the tulips by the window; they love it there. It's cold. There's no getting around the ghosts of this place. Why don't we go outside? We've got an outdoor cooking area, and the staff are making another lunch for you.

You're going to have to sleep in the barn at this rate, Corin. Your head is so big, with even more horns. We're making the front door wider, so you'll be able to go in like the rest of us. I've made breakfast the way you like it or used to like—eggs benedict with hollandaise sauce and smoked salmon, sourdough, a few garden herbs—Oh dear, that's gone already. We do have a few roast chickens on rotation, thankfully. Look, it's time I updated you on a few more things.

We've lost Old Selwyn, died last year after fifty-six years of service. The Graham twins have quit, as have the two Emilys, Hunter and Creagh; only Kevin is left of the old guard, and he's only good for a few hours at a time—sorry to mention, but his leg hasn't been the same since that time you flung him through the window. The rest of the staff —Ray, Huw, and Geoff—are new to you. I've tried my best to inform them about you. They're younger people who haven't grown up with you on the news, and they say they won't find it weird to be around the likes of us. Still, I'm not sure how tough they are. One of them jumped at a cockroach yesterday, a dead one.

We'll need to stock up more. Food's hard to come by, but we do have some crops and some livestock that haven't been stolen. Dinner's at six, so you have a few hours to wander the property, maybe get a bit of exercise. I'll go and see Kevin; my bandages are bleeding again. Do be good, will you? I know you will, but please behave. I feel this is our last chance, given my age and yours. I love you, my brother.

***

Huw said you went and slaughtered a cow. The way he described it, you would think you did it more for sport than for anger, and sadly that looks true. I'll have to pick out the entrails you left on the trees; you go to the river, wash the blood off your mouth. Then I'll wipe Huw's memories and have a rest. It's hard, you know, wiping people's minds like that— not just the energy it saps from me; I have them on my conscience now. Forgetting is my gift to them, but it costs me. I cannot forget, and so I have to keep that secret and lie every day to their faces.

Old Kevin thankfully doesn't have to be wiped; he has earned my trust and chooses to forget. He is a blessing. He feigns dementia and doesn't remember your deed in the fields today, just as he did all those times Dad questioned him about the damage we did to his car or our home. We have him to thank for learning about Father, our heavenly one. I may have heard about God in the stories Old Kevin told us, but when that man defended us, hid us, and protected us, I felt Father God was really there. It has stayed with me, and I know it stayed with you, perhaps even now? I do miss our many conversations, Corin. The sight of the carnage shocks me, and yet I have faith you're still in there.

***

Three weeks. I've forgotten how hard it was to live with you once you became the monster. I'm sitting out here on the hilltop with the radio on the news channel and wondering why the constant reports of the Plague Angel provide me with comfort, of all things. In the distance I watch another tree fall, the cockatoos screeching in protest. A cow starts screaming into the misty air, perhaps trapped by the tree or gripped by the neck with your claws. You're gargantuan now, and the killings are like your playtime. I keep the staff away from the forest; shocking I've come to think it's better you kill in the forest than near the Manor for the sake of convenience. And on the reports go of the death now covering half the country. I've decided to pray about the news as I listen but, if that's a kind of fight, then I don't know that I'm winning. I sometimes wonder if you and the Plague Angel are simply two of the same kind—mysterious beasts emerging from who knows where, angry and full of devastation. I wonder who would win in a fight. Maybe you deserve each other?

The thought of it perish. Though it's getting harder to slay such thoughts as they begin to multiply. I'm pretty old, now; if not outside, then surely within. I don't know why you were made a monster. I don't know why you didn't become human again after seven years like King Nebuchadnezzar; I suppose it was never a promise or some immutable law, though I pleaded with tears that it was. I just don't want to care anymore, but then I can't *not* care. My heart weighs with the memory of everything you've done since I brought you back—killing enough cows to make me wipe the minds of the staff to their limits, literally devouring our food reserves. The arm that has atrophied since you cut me that first day; alas, your claws are poisonous. I'm beyond blaming our parents or the system or whatever policy change put you in that asylum but, as I water the tulips in the pot, a question hangs over me that I don't want to dwell on: Why don't I give up now? The skies are full of cloud; only the cow continues to scream and then, it too, stops.

The question is a challenge. It's like that game we used to play with Old Kevin when we were little, trying to catch him out, remember? We'd ask him: "Do you believe in God?" Then we'd ask him, "If you believe in God, why do you look so unhappy?" At first, his face would fall. But then he'd grab us and tickle us till we cried, and all the while would ask us back:"Do *you* believe in God? If you believe in God, why do you look so happy?" I'd always thought it was cheeky, a copout. But now I wonder if he wasn't telling us there's no one way a child of God looks; it's what comes out of a person that matters. Old Kevin rarely did anything that didn't mean something.

You're coming back, stepping over the barbed wire fence, an unusual sign of care. Your face is splashed with river water, bits of weed tangled in your horns. You sit on the ground, sniffing the air. There you go with all that silence again. I get a sense of people, but not you, not anymore; you're an entirely different species. I've told you I don't care if you can't say the words, but sometimes I wonder if you're trying to say anything at all. The radio keeps up its chatter, with updates on the latest destroyed towns including Broken Hill, which isn't too distant from us. For a moment I think I see you looking my way, maybe to look at the tulips or listen to the radio reports but, when I turn my head, you simply lie back for a snooze, making the ground shake.

***

Thank you, Corin, for bringing the bed out. I've decided to spend my last days outside. I've had to let the staff go; their minds have been wiped enough to cause a stroke if I keep pushing it. They're in grief because dismissing them means I'm not long for living and I'm done for being served. I fare them well: give them severance, a share of whatever food is left, and a pot of red riding hoods each. It leaves them in tears, and they hug me one by one. I watch them leave on a bus to town. Old Kevin has brought me my photo albums and, of course, our own pot of tulips. He gives me a blanket, his face grim. He turns the radio on, just as the newsreader mentions death in the next valley. I close my eyes and begin to pray that God would heal this land, soul by soul.

I can't help praying about you, Corin, almost as much as everything else. I grieve, in a way, because you're not the Corin I remember—the one who protected me from Dad when Old Kevin wasn't around, taking his blows, who saw things in others they couldn't see themselves. You always did say I never saw how lovely I was in my youth, though enough boys were keen to tell me otherwise. And yet you fended them off when you knew they were trouble. Here I am looking at my old photos, and I finally see—I really was that beautiful. But what's the point of knowing it now? I regret that neither of us had children, and yet who would want children to see this life? I tell Kevin to take away the photos. It's all become too much, too sad.

I don't remember you picking me up, Corin, or when you tore my arm off like a stick. The thing was dead anyway, but even as it cartwheels away the sting in the rest of my flesh is off the scale. Some would pass out from the pain, but you put me on the ground in the arms of Old Kevin, very much awake. The blanket becomes a tourniquet, though the bleeding is surprisingly little, as if you knew just where to slice. What bleeds more is my heart as we watch you leave.

Already the vegetation on the next hill is withering, heralding the rise of the Plague Angel. It's not as I pictured it. It looks like a she: a little girl, but clearly head and shoulders taller than the trees that fall in its—her wake. The look on her face is so hungry, as if everything she wants to eat turns instead to dust. Her eyes widen at the sight of you, her equal in size, walking towards her. Old Kevin and I begin to pray, clinging tight as a dust storm throws itself towards us.

You're far away now, looking small. Your scales ripple in the sunlight; then the dust whips about you and you disappear. For a moment I could have sworn you looked like the Corin of old, your arm up to defend me once more, but that could be a trick of the mind. A strange thought—have you left to fight as a beast or a boy? The ground trembles. Then sunlight breaks through ahead, revealing a glimpse of you both, two titans in combat or maybe an embrace or both. We see the girl's mouth open, impossibly large; it bites down, tearing into your flesh. You scream, but hug the girl to you tight, your claws locked into her; and it has me in tears. Then dust takes over again, and there's nothing more.

Shoreward

JAKE DENNIS

In mem. Kerensa Allason

Flinging jellyfish from Rottnest to Freo
thundering through salt or lifting kids
from chlorine in Laverton, you set your rhythm:
andante, a gentle warrior-teacher's pace.

Breathing controlled to round the bray of oboes,
a mentor like your mother, your music lives
in shoals of swimmers' steady kicks: a vision
of graceful strength continued race to race.

Bowels fouling, cancer-stung, crying
curses against venom's goal, you fought;
remained thoughtful-tongued, unlike some dying
bitter divers in cancerous currents caught.
Refilling oceans as we leave your sight:
our storm of strokes and God's welcome light.

the sea

LYNNETTE LOUNSBURY

this is not at all who I thought I would be
alone on the morning sand watching the
ocean sweep the beach and brush away
the drunken bluebottles of the night before
I have not been alone in twenty years
I have forgotten if I like it
it feels like loss
there is a pod of dolphins terrorising
the gentle waves
poking holes in the soft skin of the sea
I think too, there is a solo swimmer
thrashing away her sins in the ice cold
another woman alone
we are all or nothing, buried or exposed
we are beached and brought to light
naked in the sun. nothing else.
this loneliness (or is it loss)
is a dangerous thing. and a gift.
there is a spotted brown octopus in the rockpool
big as a cup of tea. another woman alone.

An Unexpected Legacy

DAVE DISHMAN

Alma, the church treasurer, drummed her fingers. These elders moved through an agenda slower than the federal government. But what more could she expect from a bunch of farmers who enjoyed a summer afternoon listening to corn creaking in their fields.

The topic of conversation finally turned to the fund-raising efforts for their new church. The congregation overflowed their clapboard building, thanks to growing families and fresh followers of Jesus. Before them appeared the opportunity to build a spacious house of worship on this foundation of enthusiasm. They purchased the land months earlier, an inviting location bordered by grainfields (like every available building spot in Northern Indiana).

Alma recently returned to her hometown after years away. She brought a teenaged daughter and left a wayward husband. Alma appeared at her childhood church where a few folks silently condemned, but most extended grace. The long healing process began, one step involving her role as church treasurer—a welcome position in a rural county with few jobs at all for single, divorced moms.

As the meeting ended with a long invocation by the head elder, Alma prayed under her breath, *Lord, give me patience.* The minutes she typed promised a return to the funding question in another month, after further thought and deliberation. She respected these elders who supported her through the difficult circumstances in her life. But seriously, they moved way too slow. For good or for bad, she couldn't wait. A thought formed with the muttering of her prayer. She clipped out the door with an unorthodox idea.

Alma decided that evening to raise the rest of the money herself. She started selling baked goods and, inspired by her determination, other women fired up their ovens. Slowly her personal building fund, rising like corn in a silo, rivalled the elders'.

Alma merged her funds with those of the surprised and delighted elders. Over the next few months, a new church of red brick rose proudly in the fields. Hands trembling with joy, Alma wrote the cheque to secure the deed.

As Alma walked into the new building for meetings and services, she prayed quietly. *Dear Lord, please live in this place, bless those who come after me, and help anyone walking through the doors find you.*

A few months later, as the elders planted spring crops, Alma travelled down to Indianapolis for a doctor's visit. While crossing a busy street, an out-of-control vehicle struck her. Through several days of agony, the faithful prayed, but Alma never recovered. Holding her funeral in the church she loved, friends and family mourned a life cut short and a daughter left alone.

Eventually, Alma's daughter moved away from Indiana and started a family. She raised her two daughters far from cornfields and farther from the faith Alma found so important. At times, Alma's granddaughters studied grainy, colourless photos and wondered about their grandmother, even as friends and activities pulled them away. Beyond their knowing, a mysterious connection lingered, created by Alma's prayers years before inside that little church.

As a teenager, the younger granddaughter lived through her own accident involving an out-of-control vehicle. In the midst of tragedy, a friend introduced her to Jesus. Over the next few years, she nurtured her beliefs. She attended university, where she connected with a group of like-minded students. Her vibrant faith showed to those around her. She excitedly shared her new experiences with her sister.

Give me a break! Her older sister lashed back with arguments and ridicule. Intelligent and independent, the older sister saw no need for the crutch of religion. The God of cornfields held no place in her heart. Possessing every bit of Alma's drive, she set out on her life journey.

Eventually landing at the same university, the sisters shared an apartment and resumed their back and forth. One evening as the older mocked, the younger responded in tears and with these words from a children's song: "Jesus loves me this I know, for the Bible tells me so". Though not a serious answer for an outspoken agnostic, it was all the younger sister mustered in the face of jeers and objections.

Despite her hard exterior, the older granddaughter wrestled with the idea of faith. She questioned. She pushed back. New friends entered her life at the university, fellow students of intelligence and learning and drive, people she respected who also happened to follow Jesus.

At the height of this wrestling, the sisters drove 800 miles to a family reunion back in Indiana. Part of the festivities with aunts and uncles and cousins involved a Sunday morning service at that little church in the field. The well-worn church smelled of coffee and floor wax, appearing as nothing more than a tired building to these two bright young women of the world.

Unknown to them, the sisters walked into a church built and paid for through the efforts of their grandmother.

The younger granddaughter relaxed, looking forward to a worship service surrounded by family. Her older sister, skeptical and guarded, stepped unaware into the house of her grandmother's prayers.

The pastor took the pulpit and apologised. "Last night, I had a strange experience—God shook me out of bed and told me to preach a different sermon this morning than I originally prepared. I stayed up all night and wrote a message. I don't know who this is for, but here goes … ."

Immediately the older sister sucked in her breath. As the preacher exhorted those present to embrace the way of Jesus, her hands tremored. She listened to words delivered specifically for her, glancing at her sister in fear and amazement. Feeling bombarded, she fled from the church as the service ended. A few days later, after a thoughtful journey home, she committed to a life of faith.

Alma never dreamed that her own granddaughter would shake with conviction on pews paid for with homemade cookies. How many of Alma's prayers linger, waiting to be fulfilled in the lives of her descendants at just the right moment?

Alma would be proud to learn her older granddaughter teaches at a Christian college, and her younger granddaughter serves as a missionary. Both women raised children in the tradition of Alma, and today their children are raising a new generation in the same way—continuing a legacy of faith and family, built on the prayers of an impatient church treasurer.

Note: The author's been married to the younger granddaughter for thirty-seven years and learned of this story from Alma's nephew.

The Choir

TIM HAY

we're all singing in the choir of life
whether we choose to sing or not
do you feel discordant
or can you harmonize

it's up to us to listen
to the notes they wrote before we came along
and dwell upon the ways they might be right or wrong
reform, reshape, or keep the ancient song
to tailor make or amalgamate
and so it goes
on and on

and you decide
choose your side
in the styles and tones, the flesh and the bones
of the sound that you've been given
explore the depth of the life you're living
know the deep
know the shallow
know the water

teach your sons and teach your daughters
teach us all how you keep swimming

infinite movements
finite improvements
layer on layer
of sound for the player
spoken
sung
screamed from your lungs
breathed in your whisper
melodious hum
cacophonous
sinister
your thought
your sound
needs to be sought
needs to be found

Not a Piece of Cake

TARA WEYERS

I am turning seventeen soon, and I don't want a big fuss this year. No party at all, no presents, and definitely no big, decadent birthday cake.

I haven't always been like this. Birthday cakes have been the most memorable part of all my previous birthday parties. In my early years, birthday cakes were acts of love, made mostly by my talented grandmother. They weren't just tasty; they were also always fun. My earliest childhood memory might just be looking at my fourth birthday cake, which was in the shape of Curious George, a monkey from one of my favourite childhood shows. The cake was cut out in the shape of a monkey and had M&Ms for eyes. It was the coolest thing for me as a child.

Looking back now, it's still memorable and fun. However, I don't want that kind of cake this year, turning *seventeen*. My fifteenth birthday cake was a spectacular two-tiered chocolate cake that was sprinkled with chopped up Maltesers. It had whole Maltesers on the side of the cake, along with pink macarons. The centrepiece of the cake was fondant tennis balls, in honour of my favourite sport, filled with the sweetest, crunchiest rice krispie filling. These were a good laugh at fifteen but, two years later, I am not about to ask for anything fondant. I don't even like the taste of fondant. My sixteenth birthday cake was covered in chocolates on the top with KitKats surrounding it and, underneath, was a chocolate cake that was fluffy and delicious. All these cakes have been a hit, a reflection of all I've loved through the years. There was one, however, that didn't represent me.

It was my sixth birthday cake, my first birthday to be celebrated in Perth, Western Australia and, unbeknownst to me, my mom had planned a surprise party and a surprise cake. As I walked inside, hardly noticing the delicious smells and decorations, my mom asked me, "Does anything look different, Tara?" My eyes had grown wide and had zoned in on a big, blue, iced cake that was in the shape of a cupcake in the centre of the table. That cake shocked and disappointed my six-year-old self. *Blue icing? Seriously? There had better be chocolate cake under that blue icing!* I thought.

The party started and I went through the motions, greeting my friends, playing party games. Then came the moment of truth: the cutting of the cake. Whilst blowing out the candles, my heart was racing. It was time to see if my one birthday wish would come true: that under the blue icing was a chocolate cake. I blew out the candles and there was cheering as my mother cut the cake. My face fell. Under that blue icing was the most boring flavour. *Vanilla? Ugh! Were the Australians against chocolate?* Ah, the birthday where my biggest concern was simply a wrong-flavoured cake. If only that could be my biggest grievance this year or even the biggest grievance the second time I met this flavoured cake.

Six years later, I found myself in middle school. On a Friday in Food Tech, we did some baking. I chuckled to myself when I saw what we had to bake. Food Tech was never my favourite subject. The school was not into my taste of food, as, unlike me, it was vegetarian and all, but this was something I hadn't expected to face again: vanilla cupcakes with blue icing. *Okay, Australia, upset me once, shame on you. Upset me twice, shame on me,* I thought.

I climbed into the car after school and told my mother what we had to bake. My mother chuckled and asked if I had actually eaten it. I laughed and said that I had and it wasn't that bad. *Wow, there's some character growth. Six-year-old me would have thrown that cupcake away, but I have bigger problems now.* I kind of wish for the days when a blue-iced vanilla cupcake was my biggest problem. School was never fun. In Food Tech, my group would always make me be the clean-up person afterwards, while they criticised how I did it along the way. I had no friends at school and not so many outside of school, so a big birthday cake wasn't an issue that year.

After that reminiscing, I still don't know what to do for my seventeenth. Chocolate is the flavour that I'd want, but I am no longer a child, and not quite yet an adult. If I were about to turn fifty, who knows what I would do? That's the age where you are surely fully an adult and, perhaps, you are sick of being an adult. Perhaps you want to go back to those good old days of big, decadent, exciting things. You don't want to be plain and boring; you want to be fun and exciting. Maybe, as a fifty-year-old, I will have the cake I have dreamt up in my mind: a cake that resembles the cover of one of my books. Ironically, one main background colour of the cover of my first book *Sunflower and Her Tremendous Adventures* is blue, so the blue icing strikes again. The cake would also celebrate the book being forty years old. Now that's my dream cake. Underneath all the icing, maybe I can make it chocolate. That would be absolutely perfect!

Right now, I am sixteen; and I have turned mature and boring. This year, it's as though the child who was so excited for birthday parties and cakes has slowly slipped away and been replaced by a teen who is not wanting to celebrate the day of her birth but rather grieve the lifelong medical condition known as 'hydrocephalus' that afflicted her mere weeks before her birth. My birthday has turned into a grieving period instead of a celebration. Why would I have a cake, a sweet treat symbolizing celebration and joy, when my heart is grieving and crying out for answers as to why and how this condition fell upon me?

A cake is childish and frivolous but, maybe, that's the point. A birthday can be seen as just an ordinary day, a day that a few years ago, a child was born into life. Nothing truly changes year to year; life doesn't get much better. Consider the term 'Sweet Sixteen'. Why is sixteen so sweet? If I reflect on the past year, nothing truly changed. It wasn't any sweeter. Every year comes, as you grow up, with higher expectations of you. Life gets more stressful: less carefree, less fun and, therefore, you lose the childish joys. That includes the need for a party and cake but, maybe, that's why you should have one. To keep with the traditions of parties and cakes is to stay young. Maybe a cake's purpose is to be just that—frivolous—but in another way not. If there's one way that I recall each birthday, it's by the cakes made year to year. Cakes are timestamps; behind each one is a story, a trip down memory lane.

I know now what I will do! I will throw a tennis party to celebrate what I *am* able to do, despite this condition, and shall keep the cake so as to taste and see that the Lord is good, despite what He allowed seventeen years ago. As for what the cake would look like, I am thinking simple and small: a rectangular chocolate cake will do. As for who would make it, the one behind my early cakes, my beloved grandmother, has now passed; yet her memory lives on with each birthday, which always contains talk of her delicious, decadent cakes. My family has been spoiled the past few years with a friend making our cakes; she made the cake with the fondant tennis balls and my sixteenth but, this year, it will just be a simple and plain chocolate cake. That'll work, right?

With a background in creative writing and history, **Jackson Black** thoroughly enjoys memoir and life writing. He spends his spare time reading about the past and occasionally actually managing to put pen to paper. However, when he's not buried in ideas and words he's a passionate horseman, particularly enjoying dressage.

Ariel June Chen went to Curtin University. She enjoys exploring different parts of Perth, paying attention to the little details, and taking inspiration from the places she visits and the people she interacts with for her writing. Ariel hopes that her writing will entertain her readers and prompt reflection on the bigger implications of things brought up in her work.

Zoe Cochrane is a university student completing her bachelor's degree in Secondary Teaching at Avondale University with a specialisation in English and History. She is a long-term lover of all things literary and creative and is found most often buried in a good book, baking, or painting with her speaker blaring K-Pop tunes.

Alison Dench was born in England and moved to Australia as a child. She has always loved the sound of words. Her love of language has grown over the past thirty years while living and teaching in Australia, the Philippines, and Outer Mongolia. She currently lectures at Sheridan Institute of Higher Education, giving academic writing support to all students.

Jake Dennis @PoetOfJazz is a Burmese-Australian entertainer. **Poetry:** *Art Monthly Australia, Cordite, Crow, Cuttlefish, The Disappearing, Eastlit, Eureka Street, FourW, Mekong Review, Page Seventeen, Poetry NZ, Quadrant, Stars Like Sand, Strutco UK, Suspect NY, Voiceworks, Westerly.* **Awards:** Right Now: Human Rights Poetry Prize, Now & Then: Literature Prize, KSP Young Writer-In-Residence. **Performance:** *Beautiful Girls: Bruno Mars Show, The Glass Menagerie,* KSP Festival of Asian-Australian Voices, *Like Blown Smoke,* Madonna's *Rebel Heart* DVD, *Come Fly With Me,* Twin Cities Radio, WA Poetry Festival, Short and Sweet, Perth Poetry Club, The Wetlands Centre. BA (Communication and Cultural Studies) Curtin. www.poetofjazz.com

Stephanie Dennis is a South-African born Perth-based 1950s-style housewife. **Publications:** *Right Way Down, Into The Wetlands, Seagift.* **Screen Credits:** *Unseen Presence, Adventures of Detective Girls, Upright.* Awarded Country Girl Management's "Biggest Inspirational Girl" Runway Prize. Stephanie loves acting, animals, baking, ballet, butterflies, cinema, creative writing (memoir, poetry, stories), flowers, gardening, op-shopping, painting, sewing, singing, travelling, and the beach. Find her on Insta @stephanie_perthwamodel

Dave Dishman works with Faculty Commons, a campus ministry organisation focused on university faculty around the world. Married with three adult children and one granddaughter, he lives in Colorado after growing up in the Ozark Mountains of Southern Missouri. His two books are *GO: Following Jesus to the Ends of the Earth* and *Seers, Sayers, Schemers & Saints: Lessons on Leadership from Overlooked Men and Women of the Bible.* In his free time he enjoys the outdoors of Colorado and blogs at davedishman.com.

Tim Hay writes a lot of things and thoughts, mostly at night, and many of them don't make as much sense in the light of day but occasionally they do and that's when he feels okay about sharing them. In no particular order, he's an amateur musician, support worker, father of two, and husband of one, currently living in the Blue Mountains.

Judith Huang is an Australian-based Singaporean author, poet, literary and science fiction translator, composer, musician, serial-arts-collective-founder, Web 1.0 entrepreneur and VR creator @www.judithhuang.com. Her first novel, *Sofia and the Utopia Machine*, was shortlisted for the EBFP 2017 and Singapore Book Awards 2019. A three-time winner of the Foyle Young Poet of the Year Award, Judith graduated from Harvard University with an A.B. in English and American Literature and Language and taught creative and academic writing at the Harvard Writing Center and Yale-NUS College. She has published original work in *Prairie Schooner*, *Asia Literary Review*, *Creatrix*, *The South China Morning Post*, *The Straits Times*, *Lianhe Zaobao*, *QLRS* and *Cha* as well as being a founding member of the Spittoon Collective and magazine in China.

Mikayla Johnson is an aspiring writer who has been telling stories since she was five years old. Mikayla was born and grew up in Australia. She is currently studying creative writing at Sheridan Institute of Higher Education where she enjoys developing her creative thinking and writing skills through her studies. Mikayla likes reading a variety of fiction and is particularly keen on the genre of fantasy.

Andrew Lansdown is a widely published and award-winning Australian writer whose works include three novels, two short story collections, one essay collection, two children's poetry collections, two photography-and-poetry collections and fifteen poetry collections. His most recent book, *Abundance: New and Selected Poems* (Cascade Books, Oregon, USA), was shortlisted for the 2021 Australian Christian Book of the Year Award. His website is: www.andrewlansdown.com

Ben Lee writes short stories and creative non-fiction. His work emerges from his Chinese-Australian heritage, his faith, and the clutter around him. He has a Masters in Creative Writing from the University of Technology, Sydney (UTS) and has been published in *The UTS Writers' Anthology, Meanjin, SWAMP Online* magazine and other publications. Ben loves playing the flute and recorder by ear, racquet sports and op shopping. He has an awkward relationship with lawns.

Natalie Cher Leitão has always loved playing with words and has recently rediscovered the enjoyment of writing creatively. Inspiration struck unexpectedly in 2020 and 2021 while exploring the Pilbara and Kimberley on camping trips with her husband Rico. Natalie's day job involves writing that is formal and factual; for over two decades, research, reports, and record keeping have been the product of two-finger typing on the keyboard. Now her fingers are taking baby steps as they learn to dance to a new rhythm.

Miriam Wei Wei Lo is interested in the intersection of art and faith, how rhythm works in poetry, and Chinese diaspora autograph albums. Her most recent book of poetry is *Who Comes Calling?* She teaches creative writing at Sheridan Institute of Higher Education. Find her on Substack miriamweiweilo.substack.com

Lynnette Lounsbury is a writer, lecturer, and filmmaker who lives in Sydney, Australia. She is the author of two novels and has produced across film and television.

Samuel Mitchell is a bank clerk. He lives near a river in Eastern NSW. He is married. He and his wife have three children. He has previously had poetry published in *Studio* and *Seagift 2022*.

Amanda Poppe is passionate about the importance of reading aloud to children for literacy development. She has published an article and given speeches on this topic, but her real love is writing stories that grab the attention of adolescent boys. She can be found near Perth, WA, scouring the trees for howler monkeys or anything else she can put in her middle grade fiction.

Carolyn Rickett is a Senior Lecturer and creative arts practitioner and the Dean of Learning & Teaching at Avondale University. She is the co-editor of several poetry anthologies and her research publications include the areas of: trauma studies, writing as therapeutic intervention, cancer narratives, journalism, literary studies, poetry praxis and pedagogy, HDR supervision, healthcare chaplaincy, and professional ethics.

Tara Weyers is a young author with a passion for writing, chocolate, and cats. Life's adventures have taken her as far as Bermuda and as near as Perth in her quest for writing inspiration and the perfect blend of chocolate. Tara has self published two books so far, and is currently enjoying studying a Bachelor of Arts at Sheridan Institute of Higher Education.

Angeline Yap is an award-winning Singaporean poet whose work has appeared in literary publications and textbooks since the 1970s. Since the 1980s, she has mentored emerging writers in Singapore, served as a speaker at writing events and judged competitions for young writers. She has also collaborated with artists and writers from the USA, UK, Asia and Australia. Her poems have been read over radio and television and at literary festivals, translated into Tamil and Mandarin, and set to music for performance by choirs in Singapore and internationally.

Publisher:
Sheridan Institute of Higher Education
P.O. Box D178
Perth
WA 6849
Australia

Email: seagift@sheridan.edu.au

ISBN: 978-0-6455636-1-0

Cover image and design by Miriam Wei Wei Lo.

Seagift was curated and edited on the lands of the Whadjuk people of the Noongar nation. We acknowledge their traditional custodianship and pay our respects to their Elders.

"Many waters cannot quench love, neither can floods drown it." Song of Solomon 8:7a

www.ingramcontent.com/pod-product-compliance
Lightning Source LLC
Chambersburg PA
CBHW030418120726
47904CB00007B/2331